Silent Serenades

Eesha Alagappan

BookLeaf Publishing

India | USA | UK

Presentation by *BookLeaf Publishing*

Web: www.bookleafpub.com

E-mail: info@bookleafpub.com

ISBN: 9789367393390

First edition 2024

PREFACE

I hope you'll see a reflection of your soul in these pages. Explore the depths of strength, solitude, and immense despair in these pages.

Cocoa Rivers

In a meadow where coconut rivers flow
and chocolate trees with fudge leaves grow
Stands cake that sings, oh so sweet
and fluff clouds where gumdrop rain meets
the rivers swirl with caramel streams
A bite of chocolate will melt your dreams

Pizza Bling

2

The pizza pies are dancing high,
With pineapple stars in the sky
Cheesy moons and olive rings
Are topping the night with pizza bling
garlic parmesan sauce splashes in delight
As jalapenos twirl in cheesy flight,
Slice by slice, salty crust
Pizza every Friday Night is a must

Upon the Sea

3

Upon the sea lies unknown
Prepare to be blown
We live in worry
Our hearts aflurry
Content when we reach our destination
We don't do this because of obligation

Birthday light

Balloons floating in the air
Pink confetti's falling everywhere
The cake is topped with candles bright
The sparkly glow illuminates the light
A tiara placed on a young girls head
Dreams so bright, she bounces in bed.

Summer Magic

5

Sunshine reflected on the sea
And waves are washing up on the shore, just for
me
Popsicles melt with every lick,
And beach balls bounce in the picnic
Sunglasses shimmer, and sandcastles rise
Under the clearest of summer skies

Beachside bliss

Seagulls squawk and surfboards soar
I can hear the ocean roars
Seashells and seaweed form a line
and my tan feels just divine.
With salty air and sand so fine

Mother Earth

Mountains wear their snowy crowns
While pine trees stand as nature's gowns
The air is crisp and cool and pure
With every view, the heart secures
Rocky trails and streams that sing
Bring joy to every lost, wandering thing

Dawn

8

Whispers through the pines,
autumn leaves dance with the breeze—
nature's quiet song.

Day

9

Autumn leaves descend,
whirling in a crisp dance down—
earth's quiet farewell.

City Lights

Bright yellow cabs,
A city where dreams grab
Skyscrapers touch the sky
As taxis zoom and pigeon's fly
Hot dogs sizzle on the street
New York City's vibrant scene
It's far beyond a country gal's dream

Oh Mighty Europe

11

Cobblestone streets and café spills,
Where time stands still with ancient thrills
Chocolates melt in Paris lights
I could dance through Venice nights
In castles grand and wine so fine
London's charm is truly divine,
Greece, Rome, and Spain got tales to share
Europe, A continent beyond compare

Country Girl

Raised on farms and barns so wide,
Where hay bales stack and horses' stride,
Sunrise and sunsets paint the morning gold
In fields where wildflowers and tulips continue
to unfold.
Boots and jeans are daily wear,
With old town dreams and country air
Her laughter rings through fields so free
A country girl, wild as can be.

Fantasy Lands

In a land where magic inhales air
Whispers pass, without a care
A palace stands on mountains so high,
Hogwarts, where young wizards learn to fly

With spells that spark, and potions are brewed
In remedial potions, Harry's dreams are viewed

Beyond Thalia's Pine Tree, Camp Half-Blood
glows
Where demigods train, and adventure flows.
With mighty weapons in one's hand, and hearts
blaze
These treacherous teens face the trials of ancient
Greek, Roman, and Egyptian days

In Panem's shadows, the brave rise,
With fire in their hearts and hope in their eyes.
A Mockingjay's song, a fight for the free,
In districts united, they strive to be.

The maze looms large, a twist of fate,
Where runners race to escape their fate.
Through trials fierce and bonds that grow,
They seek the truth in the dark below.

And in the currents, lightning's spark
Michael Vey ignites the dark
With friends on his side, they dare to dream
In a world of power, a brilliant scheme

Artists of our time

In shadows, The Weeknd roars,
Once again, Adele's voice soars.
Ariana Grande shines on notes so high
Selena Gomez brings grace, and her pitch is why

Sabrina Carpenter paints dreams with a brush,
Olivia Rodrigo captures hearts in a rush.
Kesha glitter-bombs my party with flair
As Rihanna's anthems fill the air.

Chappell Roan spins tales with flair,
Taylor Swift weaves stories of despair.
Lady Gaga's style - vibrant art,
Britney Spears dances straight from her heart

Travis Scott rides the wave of a beat
Eminem's words cut deep, raw and bittersweet
Demi Lovato sings of strength and fight
Beyonce reigns, a queen shining bright

Usher dances better than our time, his claim
Jay-Z's verses spark a flame
Justin Bieber's voice, always the same

Justin Timberlake's pop echoes through time

Drake's smooth flow capture people in their
"prime"
Alicia Keys melody, a lyrical height
The magic of the 2000s, must be done right

Dua Lipa dances through poles, her face pales
white
Tate McRae's voice echoes, a delight
Billie Eilish whispers secrets in the night
Lana Del Rey's tune carries with all it's might

Snoop Dogg's flow is smooth as a breeze
Jessie J's powerhouse voice makes us feel ease
Nicki Minaj tops, breaking all the keys
Bruno Mars moves to the beat

Katy Perry lights up with anthems so bold
Maroon 5 never fails to bring goosebumps, so
cold
Ed Sheeran's lyrics share tales new and old,
Shawn Mendes strums tunes, behold.

BTS brings the world together, a rock star crew,
The Beatles' legacy timeless, forever young
Miley's evolution through decades doing go
unoticed

Shakira's hips don't lie, a fiery dance for all
Marshmello's beats light up every crowd

And Post Malone's music keeps the heartbeat
loud

In this tapestry of sound, the 2000s playlist
thrives
A legacy of music, where legends come alive

The Beauty of Many

In a world of grace and style,
Beautiful women light up every mile.
From Angelina's strength to Jennifer's glow,
Their stories lift us and help us grow.

Monica Bellucci brings pure elegance,
Natalie Portman shines with brilliance.
Irina Shayk is a stunning sight,
Anok Yai's beauty is truly bright.

Aishwarya Rai has enchanting eyes,
Deepika Padukone's charm never lies.
Alexandra Daddario's gaze is deep,
Gal Gadot inspires, making our hearts leap.

Anne Hathaway's smile lights up the night,
Meryl Streep's talent brings us delight.
Marilyn Monroe, a classic muse,
Adriana Lima, in dreams we choose.

Megan Fox has a fierce glance,
Madison Beer's voice makes us dance.
Madeline Cline and Madison Bailey shine,
Margot Robbie's grace is so fine.

Jenna Ortega is bold and strong,
Jessica Alba has stories to share all along.
Brooke Shields is a classic we adore,
Ariana Greenblatt brings new fire to explore.

Legends of the Court

Legends of the Court

In the arena's glow, where dreams take flight
Kobe's fierce spirit ignites the night

LeBron, the King, with vision so wide
A force on the court, he plays with pride

And Michael, the icon, with grace in his stride
Three legends united, the crowds guide

Kings of the Stage

21

Elvis shook the world with a rock 'n' roll flame
While Michael moonwalked, he redefined the
game.

Two icons of music, with styles apart
Forever they shine, like stars in the skies.

All the Things I Couldn't Do

Every day there's something new
Like dodging snacks that make me blue
Foods I treasure, I cannot eat
"Gluten-free, nut-free, and dairy's a treat!"

At birthday parties, I watch with a sigh
As cake and cookies just pass me by
"Is that a peanut?" I gasp in fear
My friends laugh and say, "Just stay over here!"

Can't have that pizza, it makes me wheeze
Allergies buzzing like pesky bees
Wishing for freedom to munch and to crunch
But my lunchbox is filled with a safe, bland
bunch

Dreaming of cookies, the chocolatey kind
But my allergies keep me in a bind
Oh, the things I couldn't do, it's true
But I'll just snack on my apple and stew

Trending Today

In a world where stories intertwine,
Ginny and Georgia, a bond so divine
Generations clash, with laughter and tears,
Navigating life through the hopes and fears

XO Kitty, with love on her mind
Chasing her dreams, leaving no heart behind
The Summer I Turned Pretty, a season of grace
Summer Dreams come alive in a warm space

Outer Banks calls with adventures untold,
Treasure and friendship, challenges are told
The Vampire Diaries, with hearts that ignite,
Shadows, in the depth of the night

Jackie and the Walter Boys, mischief in play
A sister's adventures, come what may
Cobra Kai rises, the past in a fight
Old rivalries sparked in a new, vibrant light

Never Have I Ever, a teenage delight
Navigating all the wrong fights
Modern Family shows us life's quirky blend
Joy in all forms, where laughter won't end

www.ingramcontent.com/pod-product-compliance
Lightning Source LLC
La Vergne TN
LVHW050303200726
843509LV00015B/3125